The Complete Book of

Handwriting

Grades K-3

W9-BCA-730

Thinking Kids™
Carson-Dellosa Publishing LLC
Greensboro, North Carolina

Thinking Kids™
Carson-Dellosa Publishing LLC
P.O. Box 35665
Greensboro, NC 27425 USA

ISBN 978-1-4838-2687-5

Table of Contents

Name_____

Let's Warm Up!

Practice by tracing the lines.

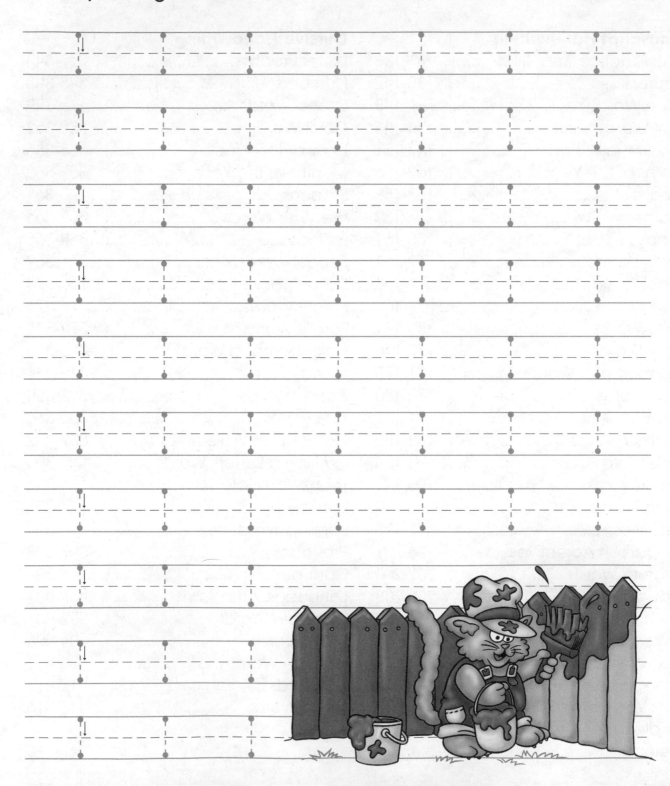

Name _____

Let's Warm Up!

Practice by tracing the lines.

Name_____

Let's Warm Up!

Practice by tracing the lines.

Name_____

Let's Warm Up!

Practice by tracing the lines.

Name_____

Let's Warm Up!

Practice by tracing the lines.

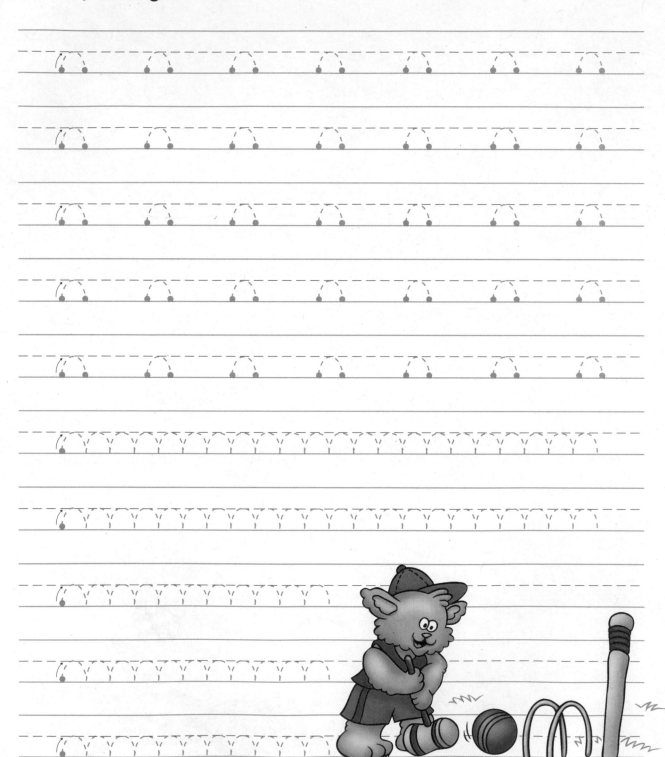

Name _____

Let's Warm Up!

Practice by tracing the lines.

Name _____

Printing Aa

Practice by tracing the letter. Then, write the letter.

Name_____

Aa

Practice by tracing the words. Then, write the words.

alligator

apple

ant

Alaska

Name_____

Aa

Write the phrases.

Alligators and ants

eat apples

Name_____

Aa

Write the sentence.

Alligators and ants
eat apples.

Aa

Write the phrases and the sentence.

Amazing Alyssa

is from Alaska

Amazing Alyssa
is from Alaska.

Bb

Practice by tracing the letter. Then, write the letter.

Name_____

Bb

Practice by tracing the words. Then, write the words.

bear

ball

bee

Bobby

Name_____

Bb

Write the phrases.

Brave Bobby

baseball bat

Name _____

Bb

Write the sentence.

Brave Bobby buys a
baseball bat.

Bb

Write the phrases and the sentence.

Bumblebees sting

beige bears

Bumblebees sting
beige bears.

Cc

Practice by tracing the letter. Then, write the letter.

Name _____

Cc

Practice by tracing the words. Then, write the words.

cats

cookies

cards

Chuck

Name _____

Cc

Write the phrases.

cool cats

play cards

Cc

Write the sentence.

Cool cats play cards.

Name _____

Cc

Write the phrases and the sentence.

Cindy cooked

chili and corn

Cindy cooked chili
and corn.

Dd

Practice by tracing the letter. Then, write the letter.

Name_____

Dd

Practice by tracing the words. Then, write the words.

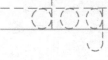
duck

dog

dance

Danny

Dd

Write the phrases.

Danny dances

dandy dog

Name_____

Dd

Write the sentence.

Danny dances with a
dandy dog.

Dd

Write the phrases and the sentence.

Dad and Dave

drew dinosaurs

Dad and Dave drew dinosaurs.

Name_____

Ee

Practice by tracing the letter. Then, write the letter.

Name_____

Ee

Practice by tracing the words. Then, write the words.

elephant

egg

elbow

Ellie

Ee

Write the phrases.

Every evening

Ellie eats eggs

Ee

Write the sentence.

Every evening Ellie eats

eggs.

Ee

Write the phrases and the sentence.

Ed the elephant

has big eyes and ears

Ed the elephant has big
eyes and ears.

Ff

Practice by tracing the letter. Then, write the letter.

Name_____

Ff

Practice by tracing the words. Then, write the words.

Ff

Write the phrases.

Four foxes

Five fish

Name_____

Ff

Write the sentence.

Four foxes and five fish fly
to Florida.

Name_____

Ff

Write the phrases and the sentence.

The flag flew

above the flowers

The flag flew above
the flowers.

Name_____

Gg

Practice by tracing the letter. Then, write the letter.

Name_____

Gg

Practice by tracing the words. Then, write the words.

giraffe

grass

glasses

Gretchen

Name_____

Gg

Write the phrases.

Gretchen wears

gray glasses

Name_____

Gg

Write the sentence.

Gretchen wears gray glasses.

Name_____

Gg

Write the phrases and the sentence.

The gray goat

eats grass

The gray goat eats

grass.

Hh

Practice by tracing the letter. Then, write the letter.

Hh

Practice by tracing the words. Then, write the words.

hippo

hat

heart

Hannah

Name _____

Hh

Write the phrases.

Hannah hears

hungry hippo

Name_____

Hh

Write the sentence.

Hannah hears a hungry
hippo.

Name _____

Hh

Write the phrases and the sentence.

The house

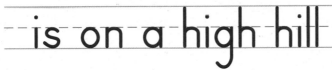

is on a high hill

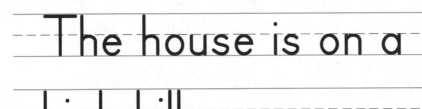

The house is on a

high hill.

Ii

Practice by tracing the letter. Then, write the letter.

Ii

Practice by tracing the words. Then, write the words.

inchworm

iguana

igloo

Indiana

Ii

Write the phrases.

Inchworms itch

in Indiana

Ii

Write the sentence.

Inchworms itch in Indiana.

Ii

Write the phrases and the sentence.

Iris had an idea

to eat ice cream on the island

Iris had an idea to eat ice
cream on the island.

Jj

Practice by tracing the letter. Then, write the letter.

Jj

Practice by tracing the words. Then, write the words.

Jj

Write the phrases.

Jumping jaguars

jolly jokes

Name_____

Jj

Write the sentence.

Jumping jaguars tell jolly jokes.

Jj

Write the phrases and the sentence.

The joker wore

jeans and jewelry

The joker wore jeans
and jewelry.

Kk

Practice by tracing the letter. Then, write the letter.

Name_____

Kk

Practice by tracing the words. Then, write the words.

kangaroo

kite

key

Kelsey

Name_____

Kk

Write the phrases.

Kind Kelsey

keeps kangaroos

Kk

Write the sentence.

Kind Kelsey keeps
kangaroos.

Name _____

Kk

Write the phrases and the sentence.

The kid wanted

a kitten and a koala

The kid wanted a kitten
and a koala.

Name _____

Ll

Practice by tracing the letter. Then, write the letter.

Name_____

Ll

Practice by tracing the words. Then, write the words.

lion

lollipop

lick

Lori

Name_____

Ll

Write the phrases.

Little Lori

likes lions

Name_____

Ll

Write the sentence.

Little Lori likes lions and
lollipops.

Name _____

Ll

Write the phrases and the sentence.

Lily licked

the lemon and lime lollipop

Lily licked the lemon and

lime lollipop.

Mm

Practice by tracing the letter. Then, write the letter.

Name_____

Mm

Practice by tracing the words. Then, write the words.

monkey

mushroom

moon

Megan

Mm

Write the phrases.

Mommy monkeys

Megan's mushrooms

Name _____

Mm

Write the sentence.

Mommy monkeys mash
Megan's mushrooms.

Name _____

Mm

Write the phrases and the sentence.

Matt needs

money for the market

Matt needs money for

the market,

Nn

Practice by tracing the letter. Then, write the letter.

Nn

Write the phrases.

Nine newts

no nest

Name_____

Nn

Write the sentence.

Nine newts have no nest.

Nn

Write the phrases and the sentence.

Nina the nurse

wrote notes

Nina the nurse wrote
notes.

Oo

Practice by tracing the letter. Then, write the letter.

Name_____

Oo

Practice by tracing the words. Then, write the words.

ostrich

octopus

olive

Olivia

Oo

Write the phrases.

Olivia owns

one ostrich

Oo

Write the sentence.

Olivia owns one ostrich and
one octopus.

Oo

Write the phrases and the sentence.

Otters often

swim in the ocean

Otters often swim in
the ocean.

Pp

Practice by tracing the letter. Then, write the letter.

Name _____

Pp

Practice by tracing the words. Then, write the words.

penguin

pizza

pencil

puppy

Pp

Write the phrases.

puppy plays

pretty pool

Pp

Write the sentence.

The puppy plays in the
pretty pool.

Pp

Write the phrases and the sentence.

Penny brought

pizza and pie to the party

Penny brought pizza and
pie to the party.

Qq

Practice by tracing the letter. Then, write the letter.

Qq

Practice by tracing the words. Then, write the words.

quail

queen

quarter

quit

Qq

Write the phrases.

quiet queen

quits quarreling

Qq

Write the sentence.

The quiet queen quits
quarreling.

Qq

Write the phrases and the sentence.

Quinn answered

the quiz questions quickly

Quinn answered the quiz questions quickly.

Name_____

Rr

Practice by tracing the letter. Then, write the letter.

R R R R R R R R R

r r r r r r r r

Rr

Practice by tracing the words. Then, write the words.

rabbit

ribbon

race

runs

Name_____

Rr

Write the phrases.

rabbits run

road race

Rr

Write the sentence.

Rowdy rabbits run a road
race.

Name_____

Rr

Write the phrases and the sentence.

The roses grew

by the railroad in the rain

The roses grew by the
railroad in the rain.

Ss

Practice by tracing the letter. Then, write the letter.

S   S   S   S   S   S   S

S   S   S   S   S   S   S

Name_____

Ss

Practice by tracing the words. Then, write the words.

seal

sun

shell

seven

Ss

Write the phrases.

Seven shells

soft sunshine

Ss

Write the sentence.

Seven shells shine in the soft sunshine.

Ss

Write the phrases and the sentence.

Six snakes

slithered under sunflowers

Six snakes slithered under sunflowers.

Tt

Practice by tracing the letter. Then, write the letter.

Tt

Practice by tracing the words. Then, write the words.

turtle

tiger

tie

teach

Tt

Write the phrases.

Ten turtles

teach tigers

Tt

Write the sentence.

Ten turtles teach tigers.

Tt

Write the phrases and the sentence.

Ted put

his toy tiger on the table

Ted put his toy tiger
on the table.

Uu

Practice by tracing the letter. Then, write the letter.

Uu

Practice by tracing the words. Then, write the words.

umpire

umbrella

under

unhappy

Uu

Write the phrases.

Unhappy umpires

ugly umbrellas

Name_____

Uu

Write the sentence.

Unhappy umpires use ugly umbrellas.

Name_____

Uu

Write the phrases and the sentence.

My uncle

was unable to clean the utensils

My uncle was unable to

clean the utensils.

Vv

Practice by tracing the letter. Then, write the letter.

Vv

Practice by tracing the words. Then, write the words.

vulture

violin

vest

van

Vv

Write the phrases.

Vultures in vests

play violins

Vv

Write the sentence.

Vultures in vests play violins.

Name_____

Vv

Write the phrases and the sentence.

Vegetables grow

on vines in a village

Vegetables grow on vines
in a village.

Ww

Practice by tracing the letter. Then, write the letter.

Ww

Practice by tracing the words. Then, write the words.

whale

walrus

water

wishes

Ww

Write the phrases.

walrus wishes

warm water

Name _____

Ww

Write the sentence.

A walrus wishes for warm water.

Ww

Write the phrases and the sentence.

The woman watched

winter from her window

The woman watched winter
from her window.

Xx

Practice by tracing the letter. Then, write the letter.

Name_____

Xx

Practice by tracing the words. Then, write the words.

x-ray

xylophone

Max

extra

Name_____

Xx

Write the phrases.

extra saxophone

extra xylophone

Xx

Write the sentence.

Max got extra xylophones
and saxophones.

Name_____

Xx

Write the phrases and the sentence.

We put the x-rays

of the fox in the box

We put the x-rays of the
fox in the box.

Yy

Practice by tracing the letter. Then, write the letter.

Yy

Practice by tracing the words. Then, write the words.

yak

yo-yo

yarn

your

Yy

Write the phrases.

Your yak

yellow yo-yo

Name _____

Yy

Write the sentence.

Your yak plays with a
yellow yo-yo.

Yy

Write the phrases and the sentence.

Your yellow yarn

is in the yard

Your yellow yarn is in
the yard.

Zz

Practice by tracing the letter. Then, write the letter.

Zz

Practice by tracing the words. Then, write the words.

zebra

zipper

zoo

zigzag

Zz

Write the phrases.

zany zebras

zigzag zoo

Name_____

Zz

Write the sentence.

Zany zebras zigzag through the zoo.

Name_____

Zz

Write the phrases and the sentence.

The zebra ate

zero zucchinis

The zebra ate zero zucchinis.

Name_____

Numbers

Practice by tracing the words and numbers. Then, write the words and numbers.

one 1

two 2

three 3

four 4

five 5

Name_____

Numbers

Practice by tracing the words and numbers. Then, write the words and numbers.

six 6

seven 7

eight 8

nine 9

ten 10

Numbers

Practice by tracing the words and numbers. Then, write the words and numbers.

eleven 11

twelve 12

thirteen 13

fourteen 14

fifteen 15

Name_____

Numbers

Practice by tracing the words and numbers. Then, write the words and numbers.

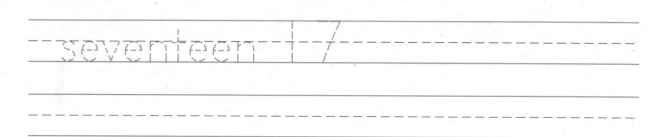

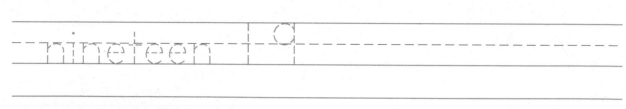

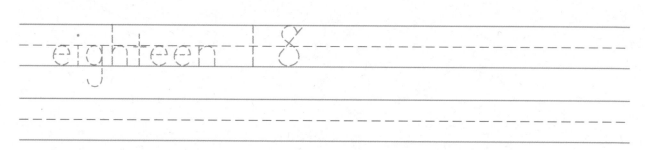

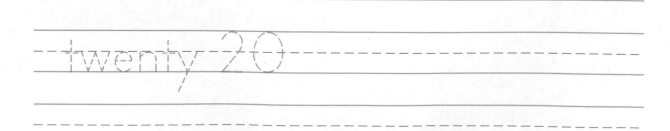

Shape Words

Practice by tracing the words. Then, write the words.

square

circle

rectangle

oval

Color Words

Practice by tracing the words. Then, write the words.

red

blue

yellow

orange

Color Words

Practice by tracing the words. Then, write the words.

black

white

purple

pink

Color Words

Practice by tracing the words. Then, write the words.

brown

gray

green

Complete this sentence:

My favorite color

is _____.

Days of the Week and Abbreviations

Practice by tracing the words and abbreviations. Then, write the words and abbreviations.

Sunday

Sun.

Monday

Mon.

Name_____

Days of the Week and Abbreviations

Practice by tracing the words and abbreviations. Then, write the words and abbreviations.

Tuesday

Tues.

Wednesday

Wed.

Days of the Week and Abbreviations

Practice by tracing the words and abbreviations. Then, write the words and abbreviations.

Thursday

Thurs.

Friday

Fri.

Name_____

Days of the Week and Abbreviations

Practice by tracing the words and abbreviations. Then, write the words and abbreviations.

Saturday

Sat.

Today

Days of the Week and Abbreviations

Complete these sentences:

Today is _____.

My birthday is _____.

The 100th day of school

is _____.

The Fourth of July is

celebrated on _____.

Name_____

Months of the Year and Abbreviations

Practice by tracing the words and abbreviations. Then, write the words and abbreviations.

January

Jan.

February

Feb.

Months of the Year and Abbreviations

Practice by tracing the words and abbreviations. Then, write the words and abbreviations.

March

Mar.

April

Apr.

Months of the Year and Abbreviations

Practice by tracing the words and abbreviations. Then, write the words and abbreviations.

May

June

July

August

Aug.

Name_____

Months of the Year and Abbreviations

Practice by tracing the words and abbreviations. Then, write the words and abbreviations.

September

Sept.

October

Oct.

Name_____

Months of the Year and Abbreviations

Practice by tracing the words and abbreviations. Then, write the words and abbreviations.

November

Nov.

December

Dec.

Seasons

Practice by tracing the words. Then, write the words.

winter

spring

summer

fall

Seasons

Complete these sentences.

Snow falls in_____.

Flowers bloom in_____.

In the_____,

we go swimming.

In the_____, leaves fall.

Weather

Practice by tracing the words. Then, write the words.

snow

rain

sunshine

sleet

Complete this sentence:

Outside I see _____.

Name_____

Holidays

Practice by tracing the words. Then, write the words.

Halloween

Easter

Fourth of July

Hanukkah

Name_____

Holidays

Practice by tracing the words. Then, write the words.

Christmas

Thanksgiving

Kwanza

Happy Birthday

Name_____

School Words

Practice by tracing the words. Then, write the words.

gym

playground

classroom

principal's office

Name_____

School Words

Practice by tracing the words. Then, write the words.

math

music

art

gym

School Words

Practice by tracing the words. Then, write the words.

science

spelling

social studies

writing

Name _____

School Words

Practice by tracing the words. Then, write the words.

teacher

aide

nurse

principal

School Words

Complete the sentences.

My teacher's name is

_____.

My school is called

_____.

My classroom is _____.

School Words

Complete the sentences.

My principal's name is

_____.

My favorite subject is

_____.

I am in grade _____.

School Tools

Practice by tracing the words. Then, write the words.

pencil

book

folder

paper

Name_____

Praise Words

Practice by tracing the words. Then, write the words.

awesome

excellent

way to go

great

Name_____

Safety Words

Practice by tracing the words. Then, write the words.

stop

go

caution

Safety Words

Complete the sentences.

A_____light means go.

A_____light means stop.

A_____light means

caution.

Family Words

Practice by tracing the words. Then, write the words.

Mother

Father

Mom

Family Words

Practice by tracing the words. Then, write the words.

Dad

Grandma

Grandpa

Name_____

Family Words

Practice by tracing the words. Then, write the words.

aunt

uncle

brother

sister

Name_____

Family Words

Write the names of the people in your family.

Neighborhood Words

Practice by tracing the words. Then, write the words.

street

road

store

theater

Neighborhood Words

Practice by tracing the words. Then, write the words.

apartment

library

office

park

Neighborhood Words

Complete the sentences.

I live in a _____.

My address is _____

Write a sentence about your neighborhood.

Name_____

Place Words

Practice by tracing the words. Then, write the words.

country

city

state

town

Place Words

Complete the sentences.

My country is _____

_____.

My state is _____

_____.

My town is _____

_____.

Food Words

Practice by tracing the words. Then, write the words.

Name_____

Food Words

Practice by tracing the words. Then, write the words.

soup

sandwich

cake

ice cream

Name

Food Words

Complete the sentences.

My favorite foods are:

If I had a restaurant,

this would be my menu:

Name_____

Direction Words

Practice by tracing the words. Then, write the words.

right

left

up

down

Name

Direction Words

Practice by tracing the words. Then, write the words.

over

under

beside

behind

Sports Words

Practice by tracing the words. Then, write the words.

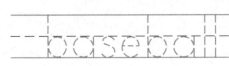

Sports Words

Practice by tracing the words. Then, write the words.

basketball

swimming

volleyball

karate

Name_____

Sports Words

Practice by tracing the words. Then, write the words.

goal

point

team

run

Sports Words

Practice by tracing the words. Then, write the words.

coach

score

guard

Complete the sentence.

My favorite sport is

●

Money Words

Practice by tracing the words. Then, write the words.

dollar $

cent ¢

penny 1¢

Money Words

Practice by tracing the words. Then, write the words.

nickel 5¢

dime 10¢

quarter 25¢

Money Words

Write the correct word under the correct coin.

_____

- - - - - - - - - - - - - - -

_____

_____

- - - - - - - - - - - - - - -

_____

_____

- - - - - - - - - - - - - - -

_____

_____

- - - - - - - - - - - - - - -

_____

_____

- - - - - - - - - - - - - - -

_____

_____

- - - - - - - - - - - - - - -

_____

_____

- - - - - - - - - - - - - - -

_____

_____

- - - - - - - - - - - - - - -

_____

_____

- - - - - - - - - - - - - - -

_____

_____

- - - - - - - - - - - - - - -

_____

Name_____

Action Words

Practice by tracing the words. Then, write the words.

run

swim

jump

fly

Name_____

Action Words

Practice by tracing the words. Then, write the words.

Adjectives

Practice by tracing the words. Then, write the words.

big

long

tall

good

Comparison Adjectives

Practice by tracing the words. Then, write the correct adjective next to each picture.

tall

taller

tallest

Comparison Adjectives

Practice by tracing the words. Then, write the correct adjective next to each picture.

big

bigger

biggest

Comparison Adjectives

Practice by tracing the words. Then, write the correct adjective next to each picture.

small

smaller

smallest

Comparison Adjectives

Practice by tracing the words. Then, write the correct adjective next to each picture.

long

longer

longest

Name_____

Comparison Adjectives

Practice by tracing the words. Then, write the correct adjective next to each picture.

good

better

best

Name_____

Comparison Adjectives

Write the comparative adjective in the blank.

I had the _____ time ever.
(best)

David is _____ than
(taller)

Susan.

It was the _____
(smallest)

kitten I had ever seen.

I ate the _____
(biggest)

ice cream sundae.

Name_____

Literature Words

Practice by tracing the words. Then, write the words.

fiction

nonfiction

biography

autobiography

Literature Words

Complete the sentences using the words given.

A _____ book
(nonfiction)

tells about things

that really

happened.

A _____ book
(fiction)

tells a story

that is not real.

A

_____
(biography)

tells the story of

someone's life.

Name_____

Math Words

Practice by tracing the words. Then, write the words.

add

subtract

multiply

divide

Name

Math Words

Practice by tracing the words. Then, write the words.

sum

product

regrouping

Complete this sentence:

When you add,
the answer is
called a _____.
(sum)

Name_____

Math Words

Practice by tracing the words. Then, write the words.

one-half

one-fourth

one-eighth

three-quarters

Math Words

Practice by tracing the words. Then, write the words.

yard

inch

foot

mile

meter

Math Words

Complete the sentences.

There are three
feet in a _____.
(yard)

There are twelve

_____ in a _____.
(inches)   (foot)

There are thirty-six
inches in a _____.
(yard)

There are 1760
yards in a _____.
(mile)

Name_____

Science Words

Practice by tracing the words. Then, write the words.

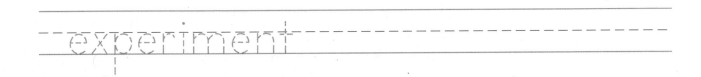

Name_____

Art Words

Practice by tracing the words. Then, write the words.

paint

draw

sketch

sculpture

Music Words

Practice by tracing the words. Then, write the words.

sing

piano

note

strings

Music Words

Practice by tracing the words. Then, write the words.

band

violin

drums

trumpet

Name_____

"Writing a Letter" Words

Practice by tracing the words. Then, write the words.

Dear

Thank you

Sincerely

Your friend

Name_____

Thank You Note

Practice writing a thank you note.

Friendly Letter

Practice writing a letter to a friend.

Envelope

Practice addressing an envelope.

Aa

Practice by tracing the letter. Then, write the letter.

a a a a a

a a a a a

Name_____

Aa

Practice by tracing the words. Then, write the words.

an

and

animals

April

Aa

Write the phrases.

Arctic animals

act amusingly

Aa

Write the sentence.

Arctic animals

act amusingly.

Name

Aa

Write the phrases and the sentence.

Annie won

an award for her model

airplane

Annie won an award

for her model airplane.

Bb

Practice by tracing the letter. Then, write the letter.

Name_____

Bb

Practice by tracing the words. Then, write the words.

big

boy

babble

baboon

Bb

Write the phrases.

Big baboons

break balloons

Name _____

Bb

Write the sentence.

Big baboons

break balloons.

Bb

Write the phrases and the sentence.

We decorated

Beth's bedroom with

birthday balloons

We decorated Beth's bedroom

with birthday balloons.

Cc

Practice by tracing the letter. Then, write the letter.

Cc

Practice by tracing the words. Then, write the words.

can

candy

cool

count

Cc

Write the phrases.

Cool crocodiles

count coconuts

Cc

Write the sentence.

Cool crocodiles

count coconuts.

Name_____

Cc

Write the phrases and the sentence.

Cathy made

cake, cookies, and cider

Cathy made cake, cookies, and cider.

Name_____

Dd

Practice by tracing the letter. Then, write the letter.

$\mathcal{D}$ $\mathcal{D}$ $\mathcal{D}$ $\mathcal{D}$ $\mathcal{D}$

d d d d d

Dd

Practice by tracing the words. Then, write the words.

do

dog

dandelions

donuts

Name _____

Dd

Write the phrases.

Dogs deliver

dandelions and

donuts

Name _____

Dd

Write the sentence.

Dogs deliver dandelions and donuts.

Dd

Write the phrases and the sentence.

Dylan likes

deer, ducks, and dolphins

Dylan likes deer, ducks, and dolphins.

Name

Ee

Practice by tracing the letter. Then, write the letter.

Name _____

Ee

Practice by tracing the words. Then, write the words.

each

eat

eels

eighty

Name _____

Ee

Write the phrases.

Electric eels

eat excitedly

Ee

Write the sentence.

Electric eels eat

excitedly.

Ee

Write the phrases and the sentence.

Eagles and elephants

live on Earth

Eagles and elephants live on Earth.

Ff

Practice by tracing the letter. Then, write the letter.

Name_____

Ff

Practice by tracing the words. Then, write the words.

far

fat

fluff

feast

Name_____

Ff

Write the phrases.

Flamingos fluff

fancy feathers

Name_____

Ff

Write the sentence.

Flamingos fluff fancy feathers.

Ff

Write the phrases and the sentence.

The fairy flew

over the flowers

The fairy flew over the flowers.

Gg

Practice by tracing the letter. Then, write the letter.

Name_____

Gg

Practice by tracing the words. Then, write the words.

gag

gift

good

giggle

Gg

Write the phrases.

Giggling gophers

gag gifts

Gg

Write the sentence.

Giggling gophers give gag gifts.

Name _____

Gg

Write the phrases and the sentence.

The goat and the giraffe

were by the gate

The goat and the giraffe
were by the gate.

Name_____

Hh

Practice by tracing the letter. Then, write the letter.

Hh

Practice by tracing the words. Then, write the words.

his

happy

he

hello

Hh

Write the phrases.

Happy hippos

hang hammocks

Hh

Write the sentence.

Happy hippos hang in their hammocks.

Name_____

Hh

Write the phrases and the sentence.

The hen and the horse

live by the house

The hen and the horse

live by the house.

Ii

Practice by tracing the letter. Then, write the letter.

Ii

Practice by tracing the words. Then, write the words.

if

in

idea

itch

Ii

Write the phrases.

Insects itch

in the infield

Ii

Write the sentence.

Insects itch in the infield.

Ii

Write the phrases and the sentence.

The island has

ice and ivy

The island has ice

and ivy.

Jj

Practice by tracing the letter. Then, write the letter.

Jj

Practice by tracing the words. Then, write the words.

jam

job

jazz

junk

Name_____

Jj

Write the phrases.

Juggling jaguars

to jazz

Jj

Write the sentence.

Juggling jaguars jam to jazz.

Name_____

Jj

Write the phrases and the sentence.

Jan bought

a jug of juice

Jan bought a jug of juice.

Kk

Practice by tracing the letter. Then, write the letter.

Kk

Practice by tracing the words. Then, write the words.

kid

key

kick

keep

Name_____

Kk

Write the phrases.

Kooky kangaroos

kick karate

Name_____

Kk

Write the sentence.

Kooky kangaroos kick in karate.

Kk

Write the phrases and the sentence.

The kids wanted

a kitten, a kite, and a kazoo

The kids wanted a kitten, a kite, and a kazoo.

Ll

Practice by tracing the letter. Then, write the letter.

Ll

Practice by tracing the words. Then, write the words.

low

land

lamb

little

Name _____

Ll

Write the phrases.

Little lambs

lemon lollipops

Name _____

Ll

Write the sentence.

Little lambs lick lemon lollipops.

Ll

Write the phrases and the sentence.

The ladybug landed

on the leaf by the ladder

The ladybug landed on the leaf by the ladder.

Mm

Practice by tracing the letter. Then, write the letter.

m m m m m

m m m m m

Mm

Practice by tracing the words. Then, write the words.

mad

milk

monkeys

merry

Mm

Write the phrases.

Merry monkeys

make marmalade

Name_____

Mm

Write the sentence.

Merry monkeys
make marmalade.

Mm

Write the phrases and the sentence.

My mom mopped

up the milk

My mom mopped up the milk.

Nn

Practice by tracing the letter. Then, write the letter.

Nn

Practice by tracing the words. Then, write the words.

nap

name

near

night

Name_____

Nn

Write the phrases.

Naughty gnats

never nap

Name _____

Nn

Write the sentence.

Naughty gnats never nap at night.

Name_____

Nn

Write the phrases and the sentence.

Nina wrote

nine notes to Ned

Nina wrote nine notes
to Ned.

Oo

Practice by tracing the letter. Then, write the letter.

Oo

Practice by tracing the words. Then, write the words.

out

often

once

order

Name _____

Oo

Write the phrases.

Ostriches often

onion omelettes

Oo

Write the sentence.

Ostriches often order onion omelettes.

Oo

Write the phrases and the sentence.

Olivia saw

an orange octopus and
an owl

Olivia saw an orange
octopus and an owl.

Pp

Practice by tracing the letter. Then, write the letter.

Pp

Practice by tracing the words. Then, write the words.

pan

pet

pick

paper

Name_____

Pp

Write the phrases.

Pandas paint

pictures paper

Name

Pp

Write the sentence.

Pandas paint pictures on paper.

Pp

Write the phrases and the sentence.

Penny wrote

a paper about penguins

and parrots

Penny wrote a paper about

penguins and parrots.

Name _____

Qq

Practice by tracing the letter. Then, write the letter.

Q   Q   Q   Q   Q

q   q   q   q   q

Qq

Practice by tracing the words. Then, write the words.

quit

quick

quart

quiet

Qq

Write the phrases.

Quick quails

unique quarter

Qq

Write the sentence.

Quick quails quarrel over a unique quarter.

Qq

Write the phrases and the sentence.

The queen asked

a quiet question about the

quilt

The queen asked a quiet

question about the quilt.

Rr

Practice by tracing the letter. Then, write the letter.

Rr

Practice by tracing the words. Then, write the words.

rat

run

rear

road

Name _____

Rr

Write the phrases.

Raccoons run

red cars

Rr

Write the sentence.

Raccoons run races in red cars.

Rr

Write the phrases and the sentence.

The rabbit

crossed the railroad in the

rain

The rabbit crossed the

railroad in the rain.

Ss

Practice by tracing the letter. Then, write the letter.

Name_____

Ss

Write the phrases.

Standing storks

sing swans

Ss

Write the sentence.

Standing storks sing with swans.

Name_____

Ss

Write the phrases and the sentence.

Seahorses and seals

swim in the sun

Seahorses and seals swim in the sun.

Tt

Practice by tracing the letter. Then, write the letter.

Name_____

Tt

Practice by tracing the words. Then, write the words.

the

tip

told

twist

Tt

Write the phrases.

Two tigers

tickle toes

Name_____

Tt

Write the phrases and the sentence.

The turtle and tortoise

are under the tree

The turtle and tortoise
are under the tree.

Name

Uu

Practice by tracing the letter. Then, write the letter.

Name_____

Uu

Practice by tracing the words. Then, write the words.

use

under

until

unhappy

Uu

Write the phrases.

Unicorns use

umbrellas under

Uu

Write the sentence.

Unicorns use umbrellas under thunder.

Uu

Write the phrases and the sentence.

The umpire wore

a shirt under his uniform

The umpire wore a shirt under his uniform.

Vv

Practice by tracing the letter. Then, write the letter.

Name_____

Vv

Practice by tracing the words. Then, write the words.

very

vote

vine

vest

Name_____

Vv

Write the phrases.

Vultures vacuum

velvet vests

Vv

Write the sentence.

Vultures vacuum in velvet vests.

Vv

Write the phrases and the sentence.

Vivian has

a van of vegetables

Vivian has a van of vegetables.

Ww

Practice by tracing the letter. Then, write the letter.

Ww

Practice by tracing the words. Then, write the words.

wet

west

wall

winter

Ww

Write the phrases.

Wet walruses

to win

Ww

Write the sentence.

Wet walruses

bowl to win.

Ww

Write the phrases and the sentence.

We could see

whales from the window

We could see whales from

the window.

Name

Xx

Practice by tracing the letter. Then, write the letter.

Xx

Practice by tracing the words. Then, write the words.

x-ray

box

extra

xylophone

Name_____

Xx

Write the phrases.

x-ray boxes

with foxes

Xx

Write the sentence.

Xandra x-rays

boxes with foxes.

X-RAY MACHINE

FOX IN BOX

Xx

Write the phrases and the sentence.

Xavier plays

the xylophone

Xavier plays the xylophone.

Yy

Practice by tracing the letter. Then, write the letter.

Name_____

Yy

Practice by tracing the words. Then, write the words.

you

yard

year

yellow

Name _____

Yy

Write the phrases.

Yaks yell

Yodel loudly

Name_____

Yy

Write the sentence.

Yaks yell and yodel loudly.

Yy

Write the phrases and the sentence.

The yak

yelled and yawned

The yak yelled and yawned.

Zz

Practice by tracing the letter. Then, write the letter.

Zz

Practice by tracing the words. Then, write the words.

zero

zoom

zone

zipper

Zz

Write the phrases.

zigzagging zebras

zip zoom

Zz

Write the sentence.

Zigzagging zebras

zip and zoom.

Name _____

Zz

Write the phrases and the sentence.

Zach has

zero zucchinis

Zach has zero
zucchinis.

Numbers

Practice by tracing the words and numbers. Then, write the words and numbers.

one 1

two 2

three 3

four 4

five 5

Name_____

Numbers

Practice by tracing the words and numbers. Then, write the words and numbers.

six 6

seven 7

eight 8

nine 9

ten 10

Numbers

Practice by tracing the words and numbers. Then, write the words and numbers.

eleven 11

twelve 12

thirteen 13

fourteen 14

fifteen 15

Name _____

Numbers

Practice by tracing the words and numbers. Then, write the words and numbers.

sixteen 16

seventeen 17

eighteen 18

nineteen 19

twenty 20

Shape Words

Practice by tracing the words. Then, write the words.

square

circle

rectangle

oval

Name

Color Words

Practice by tracing the words. Then, write the words.

red

blue

yellow

orange

Name _____

Color Words

Practice by tracing the words. Then, write the words.

black

white

purple

pink

Name _____

Color Words

Practice by tracing the words. Then, write the words.

brown

gray

green

Complete the sentence.

My favorite color

is _____.

Days of the Week and Abbreviations

Practice by tracing the words and abbreviations. Then, write the words and abbreviations.

Sunday

Sun.

Monday

Mon.

Name_____

Days of the Week and Abbreviations

Practice by tracing the words and abbreviations. Then, write the words and abbreviations.

Tuesday

Tues.

Wednesday

Wed.

Name_____

Days of the Week and Abbreviations

Practice by tracing the words and abbreviations. Then, write the words and abbreviations.

Thursday

Thurs.

Friday

Fri.

Days of the Week and Abbreviations

Practice by tracing the words and abbreviations. Then, write the words and abbreviations.

Saturday

Sat.

Today

Name_____

Months of the Year and Abbreviations

Practice by tracing the words and abbreviations. Then, write the words and abbreviations.

March

Mar.

April

Apr.

Months of the Year and Abbreviations

Practice by tracing the words and abbreviations. Then, write the words and abbreviations.

May

June

July

August

Aug.

Months of the Year and Abbreviations

Practice by tracing the words and abbreviations. Then, write the words and abbreviations.

September

Sept.

October

Oct.

Name_____

Months of the Year and Abbreviations

Practice by tracing the words and abbreviations. Then, write the words and abbreviations.

November

Nov.

December

Dec.

Seasons

Practice by tracing the words. Then, write the words.

winter

spring

summer

fall

Weather Words

Practice by tracing the words. Then, write the words.

snow

rain

sunshine

sleet

Today we have

Name_____

Weather Words

Practice by tracing the words. Then, write the words.

thunder

hail

cloudy

windy

foggy

Name_____

Holidays

Practice by tracing the words. Then, write the words.

Halloween

Easter

Fourth of July

Hanukkah

Holidays

Practice by tracing the words. Then, write the words.

Christmas

Thanksgiving

Kwanza

Happy Birthday

Name_____

School Words

Practice by tracing the words. Then, write the words.

gym

playground

classroom

principal's office

Name_____

School Words

Practice by tracing the words. Then, write the words.

math

music

art

gym

School Words

Practice by tracing the words. Then, write the words.

science

spelling

social studies

writing

School Words

Practice by tracing the words. Then, write the words.

teacher

aide

nurse

principal

Name_____

School Tools

Practice by tracing the words. Then, write the words.

pencil

book

folder

paper

Name_____

Safety Words

Practice by tracing the words. Then, write the words.

stop

go

caution

Family Words

Practice by tracing the words. Then, write the words.

Mother

Father

Mom

Name _____

Family Words

Practice by tracing the words. Then, write the words.

Dad

Grandma

Grandpa

Family Words

Practice by tracing the words. Then, write the words.

aunt

uncle

brother

sister

Family Words

Write the names of the people in your family.

Neighborhood Words

Practice by tracing the words. Then, write the words.

street

road

store

theater

Name

Neighborhood Words

Practice by tracing the words. Then, write the words.

apartment

library

office

park

Neighborhood Words

Complete the sentences.

I live in a

_____ .

My address is

_____ .

Write a sentence about your neighborhood.

Money Words

Practice by tracing the words. Then, write the words.

dollar $

cent ¢

penny ¢

Money Words

Practice by tracing the words. Then, write the words.

nickel 5¢

dime 10¢

quarter 25¢

Money Words

Practice by tracing the words. Then, write the words.

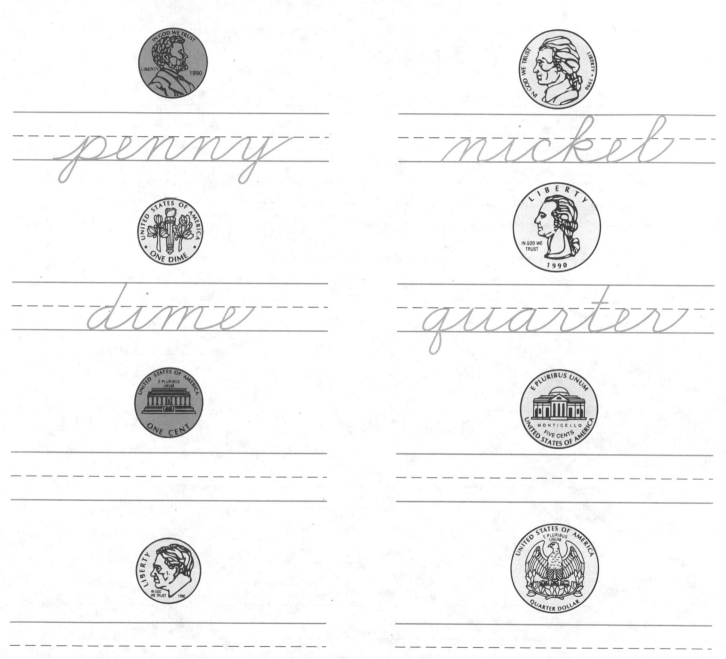

penny

nickel

dime

quarter

Name_____

Action Words

Practice by tracing the words. Then, write the words.

run

swim

jump

fly

Action Words

Practice by tracing the words. Then, write the words.

sing

read

play

study

Action Words

Practice by tracing the words. Then, write the words.

dance

walk

paint

skip

Adjectives

Practice by tracing the words. Then, write the words.

big

long

tall

good

Name_____

Adjectives

Practice by tracing the words. Then, write the words.

small

short

bad

green

Comparison Adjectives

Practice by tracing the words. Then, write the correct adjective next to each picture.

tall

taller

tallest

Name_____

Comparison Adjectives

Practice by tracing the words. Then, write the correct adjective next to each picture.

big

bigger

biggest

Name_____

Comparison Adjectives

Practice by tracing the words. Then, write the correct adjective next to each picture.

small

smaller

smallest

_____

_____

_____

Name _____

Comparison Adjectives

Practice by tracing the words. Then, write the correct adjective next to each picture.

long

longer

longest

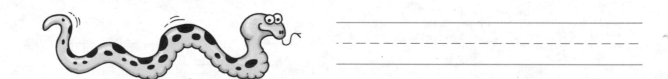

Comparison Adjectives

Practice by tracing the words. Then, write the correct adjective next to each picture.

good

better

best

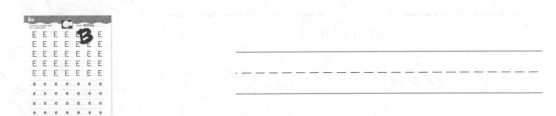

Comparison Adjectives

Write the adjective in the blank.

I had the _____
(best)

time ever.

David is _____
(taller)

than Susan.

It was the

_____ kitten
(smallest)

I had ever seen.

I ate the _____
(biggest)

ice cream sundae.

Name _____

"Writing a Letter" Words

Practice by tracing the words. Then, write the words.

Dear

Thank you

Sincerely

Your friend

Thank You Note

Practice writing a thank you note.

Name_____

Friendly Letter

Practice writing a letter to a friend.

Name_____

Spelling Words

Practice by tracing the words. Then, write the words.

dictionary

definition

alphabetical order

Name_____

Pronouns

Practice by tracing the words. Then, write the words.

I

me

you

her

we

Name_____

Pronouns

Practice by tracing the words. Then, write the words.

he

she

they

them

Contractions

Practice by tracing the words. Then, write the words.

I'll

she'll

we'll

you'll

Name_____

Language Arts Words

Practice by tracing the words. Then, write the words.

sentence

paragraph

poem

story

Name_____

Language Arts Words

Complete the sentences with the words given.

At the end of a

_____, you

(sentence)

put a period.

A _____

(paragraph)

has a main idea.

A _____ does not

(poem)

have to rhyme.

A _____ has a

(story)

beginning, a middle,

and an end.

Literature Words

Practice by tracing the words. Then, write the words.

fiction

nonfiction

biography

autobiography

Name_____

Literature Words

Complete the sentences using the words given.

A _____ book
(nonfiction)

tells about things

that really

happened.

A _____ book
(fiction)

tells a story

that is not real.

A _____
(biography)

tells the story of

someone's life.

Name_____

Math Words

Practice by tracing the words. Then, write the words.

add

subtract

multiply

divide

Math Words

Practice by tracing the words. Then, write the words.

sum

product

regrouping

Complete the sentence using the word given.

When you add,

the answer is

called a _____.

(sum)

Math Words

Practice by tracing the words. Then, write the words.

one-half

one-fourth

one-eighth

three-quarters

Math Words

Practice by tracing the words. Then, write the words.

yard

inch

foot

mile

meter

Name_____

Math Words

Complete the sentences using the words given.

There are three
feet in a _____.
(yard)
There are twelve
_____ in a _____.
(inches)   (foot)
There are thirty-
six inches in a
_____.
(yard)
There are 1760
yards in a _____.
(mile)

Name_____

Science Words

Practice by tracing the words. Then, write the words.

habitat

experiment

food chain

water cycle

Name _____

Science Words

Practice by tracing the words. Then, write the words.

gas

solid

liquid

evaporation

Name _____

Science Words

Practice by tracing the words. Then, write the words.

herbivore

energy

cells

organisms

Art Words

Practice by tracing the words. Then, write the words.

paint

draw

sketch

sculpture

Name_____

Art Words

Practice by tracing the words. Then, write the words.

color

trace

paint

cut

Art Words

Practice by tracing the words. Then, write the words.

fold

clay

color

canvas

Name_____

Music Words

Practice by tracing the words. Then, write the words.

sing

piano

note

strings

Music Words

Practice by tracing the words. Then, write the words.

band

violin

drums

trumpet